Home Inspection Answer Guide

for Buyers, Sellers, Owners, and Agents

**PROTECT YOUR INVESTMENT
AND
AVOID SURPRISES**

Lisa Turner

Turner Creek

Hayesville NC

"This enjoyable book gives home buyers and owners the tools to have the best home without unnecessary trauma and expense. No homeowner should be without it."

July 18, 2021

Brian Tracy, CEO of *Brian Tracy International*, has consulted for more than 1,000 companies, presented to more than 5 million people in more than 80 countries, and written more than 80 books.

Lisa's 2020 book, Your Simplest Life, includes a free journal. Scan the QR code below for information.

Lisa Turner's Other Books

Copyright © 2021 by Lisa Turner

All rights reserved. This book or parts thereof may not be reproduced in any form, stored in any retrieval system, or transmitted in any form by any means—electronic, mechanical, photocopy, recording, or otherwise—without prior written permission of the publisher, except as provided by United States of America copyright law. For permission requests, write to the publisher, Turner Creek.

Note to Reader: The information, tips, and advice in this book come from the author's own education, observations, and informal research. The content provided here is for educational purposes and does not take the place of professional advice. Every effort has been made to ensure that the content is accurate and helpful for readers at publishing time. However, this is not an exhaustive treatment of the subjects. No liability is assumed for losses or damages due to the information provided. You are responsible for your own choices, actions, and results.

Turner Creek Publishing
515 Barlow Fields Drive
Hayesville, NC 28904

Home Inspection Answer Guide/Lisa Turner —1st edition
ISBN: Hardback: 978-1-7366328-3-3
ISBN: Paperback: 978-1-7366328-2-6

To Jerry

❝ I wriggled through the twenty-inch square opening and onto the dirt floor. I held up the flashlight. In the arc of yellow light floated dust particles and whispery cobweb threads. Large wolf spiders stood their ground in the spaces between the beams only inches above my head. I noted the fallen insulation to my left, where I knew snakes like to sleep. The stillness was only broken by the sound of dripping water in the distance.

Crawling slowly on my belly, I quietly passed the insulation pile and headed for the black pool of water at the far end. I crawled past fallen insulation squares, mouse carcasses, and pieces of plastic sheeting. Out of the corner of my eye I caught movement to my right. Rotating my light beam, I was startled to see three pairs of reflective yellow circles move and then stop. Raccoons. I heard a chittering, snarling, sound.

I noticed the yellow cast of my flashlight beginning to falter. Then I heard the tiny door behind me slam shut and the scraping metal of the padlock on the hasp.

Trapped. **❞**

Contents

Note to the Reader xi
Introduction: Why You Need this Book 1
Chapter 1: What Buyers Need to Know 5
Chapter 2: What Sellers Need to Know 11
Chapter 3: What Owners Need to Know .. 15
Chapter 4: What Agents Need to Know 21
Chapter 5: What Builders Need to Know . 31
Chapter 6: Choosing an Inspector 41
Chapter 7: Top Five Inspection Myths 49
Chapter 8: How to Use the Report 53
Chapter 9: Additional Inspections 57
Chapter 10: Radon Facts 61
Chapter 11: True Stories 65
Chapter 12: The Quiz 81
Questions and Answers 89
INDEX 119
Notes 125
Complimentary Quizzes and Articles 126

> We love what we do. Every inspection is an adventure with mysteries to solve. We love every part of it, including the hard-to-see places—because that is where no one else is looking. The tougher it is, the more we revel in our ability to find what's wrong and what's right.
>
> Although we enjoy good homes with few problems, we get a thrill when we find a serious problem that would have bitten the next owner. We like to think we are saving people both trauma and money.

~ Lisa Turner

Note to the Reader

Why this book, and why now?

I encounter misconceptions of all kinds as a home inspector. They persist today. Do real estate agents really have a list of inspectors that will go "easy" on a home? Is it true that inspectors can identify termites through a technique called wall tapping? Do inspectors grade the home for buyers? Are code violations the most serious problem a home can have?

Confusion around what an inspector can and cannot do, the importance of attending the inspection, and what to do if your inspector misses something (or you think they did) are some of the queries.

Why not assemble a short and simple book that provides straightforward answers to each group involved in a home inspection?

Here it is.

Buying, building, selling, or owning a home can be infused with financial shocks. Getting a home inspection is inexpensive protection against wallet-opening surprises.

My aim is to save you money and aggravation. If you have all the answers, you'll be in a position to get the best deal on your home, and on your inspection.

I'll cover how you can find the best inspector; how you can build the best, most efficient home; how to use a home inspection report as a seller; why you should attend the inspection, and how to use a home inspection report to save money on maintenance. I'll also cover common home inspection myths and tell you a few scary stories.

> Water dripped down the walls of the narrow passageway, obsidian-colored rock hewn out of the cliff face. I could see the furrows where blasting caps had been used. I was feeling uncertain. Should I keep going? The dirt path was uneven and the walls were getting narrower as I made my way down the slippery incline. I heard a hissing sound as my flashlight made out a heavy closed door, blocking my way. *Go back*, my brain commanded. *Go back*.

"My house is my refuge, an emotional piece of architecture, not a cold piece of convenience." ~ Luis Barragan

Introduction: Why You Need this Book

A home is our retreat from the wild vortex of the world. A home is a secure and emotionally rewarding space in which to unwind, a place to re-energize, a place to regain composure and calm. A home returns our equilibrium and allows us to create, to thrive, to love, and to share.

When something goes wrong in our home, it sets off fundamental alarms. Much of what goes wrong can be either prevented or predicted. I don't know about you, but I hate surprises that aren't fun ones. Roof leaks are not fun. Losing hot water is not fun. Bats in the attic are not fun.

Plumbing leaks are not fun. Electrical box fuses blowing are not fun.

The answer? A home inspection.

What a home inspection does for a buyer (and everyone else, which I'll cover later) is help save them from financial and emotional trauma. I can tell you stories of buyers skipping the inspection and then calling an inspector later to find out why the deck fell off the back of the house, or why the gas furnace exploded. A home inspection's value lies in letting you know what surprises lurk in plain sight before you buy the home.

There are three other circumstances where getting a home inspection will save you from surprise and spending money: selling your home, building a home, and when you need a general assessment after years of living in your home.

As a seller, wouldn't you like to know ahead of time what the buyer is going to see in their own report? I would. If there is anything serious (the surprise), you then have the opportunity to fix what's wrong, giving you a leg up on the competition. Most inspectors will also give you a lower price on a seller inspection.

If you are building a home, I recommend a series of inspections. The inspections are insurance that the builder doesn't mistakenly introduce problems during the build. Builders have the goal to build a safe, high-quality home for you; however, I have seen everything from decks being installed incorrectly to structural piers not being located directly and securely underneath the structure they are supposed to support.

One day I visited a large building project where an elevated walkway was being installed. I noticed four walkway posts located halfway on and halfway off the concrete supports they had poured the previous week. I asked the contractor what had happened.

"Well, we made a calculation error locating the supports. We poured them in the wrong places and didn't catch the error until the posts went in. There's nothing we can do about it now." The contractor looked at me sheepishly and cocked his head.

I cleared my throat. "Yes, there is. You can pour new supports where they are supposed to be. The walkway was engineered to have fully supported posts." I pointed to one of the posts that had just been attached to the outer third of a support pad. Half of the post hung in the air.

"No one will see it; it gets covered with a façade," said the contractor. "All this is over-engineered anyway."

I shook my head. "That's even worse," I said, snapping photos. I watched as the contractor squeezed his eyes shut and swung his head from side to side.

"Ugh. What a mess. You're right. Okay."

I left the job site thinking about what would have happened had I not inspected the site that day.

Don't get me wrong. I'm not saying builders purposefully make errors. Builders perform the best job they can, but building a residence or commercial building is complex and takes many different crews to contribute to the whole. It only takes a few untrained workers and misunderstandings to create errors that ripple through the rest of the construction.

Finally, a home inspection comes in handy after you move into the home. Get another inspection five years later and compare conditions. What shape are systems in? Have any problems cropped up? What should you budget for over the next five to ten years? Are there any safety issues you should know about?

Here are the answers to your questions.

> "By George!" cried the inspector. "How did you ever see that?" Because I looked for it.
> ~ Arthur Conan Doyle

Chapter 1: What Buyers Need to Know

You've located your perfect home. Your offer has been accepted. Is this home everything you think it is? When your agent asks you if you want to get a home inspection, your answer should be, "Yes." Here are some tips to maximize your home inspection results.

Get the best inspector. A competent inspector will catch major problems in a home, and be able to put the smaller issues into perspective for you so that you can make decisions. Your inspector should be licensed and/or certified at what they do, and have a high experience level. Your agent may give you several names; either call each one or research them through their websites. The best inspector and the worst inspector will likely charge you the same amount of money, so why not maximize your return?

Some home inspection books advise you to choose your own inspector over the choices your real estate broker offers you. I don't agree with this. I believe a competent and licensed inspector will be ethical and not gloss over defects so that the agent can get a sale. Does this ever happen? I expect that it does, but in my experience, it's very rare. If an inspector purposefully leaves defects out of a report, it may return to bite them. They know that.

Be there for the inspection. Eighty-five percent of home buyers are not present during the inspection, thinking that they will disturb the inspector. Inspectors will tell you that this is not true. Tell the inspector that you will show up at the end of the inspection, and you will expect some show and tell. This gives you the best of both worlds—a happy inspector left alone to do their job, and your full understanding of the issues when they are done.

When you're at the home with the inspector, you will get an overall feeling from them about the home. This is hard to describe, and you can't get this "sense" from the written report. In listening to the inspector, you'll get much more information and between-the-lines information than you would otherwise.

If you can't be at the home during the inspection, arrange for a call with your inspector after the inspection to discuss the items. The inspector will tell you things over the phone that are not in the report. It's not as good as being there, but it's much better than only reading the final report.

Maintenance advice. Although not part of the formal inspection, most inspectors will tell you what items in the home require regular maintenance and will tell you what that maintenance roughly consists of. Examples include filter changes, heating, ventilation, and cooling (HVAC) service intervals, keeping the condensate line unplugged, etc. This is one more reason to show up for the walk-around. Take advantage of the inspector's expertise, and take notes.

Ask for referrals. Who does the inspector recommend for repairs? This is also something you will not see in the formal report, but the inspector will have a few very talented tradespeople that they use and you should find out who these people are. Inspectors do not give you referrals because it could be seen as a conflict of interest. This is the correct protocol, but face to face they may share the names of their trusted tradespeople with you.

Other inspections. One inspection that your home inspector is not qualified to do is a WDO (Wood Destroying Organisms), or termite inspection. They will notice and mention what they see, but they are not licensed to report on infestations and what to do about them.

Termites cause substantial structural damage to homes. You should employ a pest professional to inspect and report on termites and other infestations. I have seen homeowners skip the termite inspection and then have to tear out sections of the home and re-build. On one inspection I did, I noticed termite damage but was unable to determine if it was active or past activity. I put this in the report, advised getting a professional pest inspection, and I also advised the buyers about getting a WDO pro on the walk-around. Their response was, "Billy, our nephew, is going to do that."

"Billy is a licensed pest inspector?" I inquired.

"No, but he knows what to look for."

I highlighted my advice on getting a pest professional in the report before turning it over.

A month later the real estate agent who had handled the transaction pulled me aside at another inspection.

"Remember the sixty-year-old home you inspected and found termite damage in the basement?"

"I sure do."

"Three interior walls collapsed right after they moved in."

"No!"

"Yes. They never got the pest inspection."

I was dumbfounded.

Radon. Get a radon inspection if you're buying in an area of the country where this radioactive gas is known to be high. It is second behind smoking cigarettes as a cause of lung cancer. Your agent will know what the general levels are in the areas where they are selling and if it's recommended. See chapters nine and ten.

"Secrets are made to be found out with time."
~ Charles S. Sanford, Jr.

Chapter 2: What Sellers Need to Know

We think of home inspections as the tool the buyer uses to assess whether they should buy a house. But a home inspection can be an amazing tool when you are selling a home. Wouldn't you want to know in advance what possible surprises lurk in your own home that you didn't know about? Here are the pros and cons.

Getting a seller's home inspection is a good idea if:

- You want to avoid the last-minute surprises of a buyer's home inspection. Sometimes both parties are very surprised at what is found in an inspection. Suddenly there is work, aggravation, and a small measure of irrationality thrown in as both parties wrestle with who will do what. Sometimes unanticipated discoveries will sink the deal. If you have the chance to address these beforehand, you are more likely to keep the sale.

- If you want an extra edge in marketing the home. Any extra effort or component to make the home more appealing to buyers will help set your home apart from everyone else's. Getting an inspection indicates to potential buyers that you are serious about taking care of the home, and you are selling it with all issues disclosed.
- The home is already in good condition. A home inspection will probably turn up some items that you are unaware of. They may be small items and you can take care of them relatively easily. The inspection report then becomes a marketing tool.

Getting a seller's home inspection may not be a good idea if:
- You know that there are numerous problems with the home and would rather not dig up the details on them. This is a little ostrich-like, but some sellers feel that it is better to not disclose defects and rely on the "buyer beware" doctrine even though they know

there may be ramifications at due diligence time.

- The home has very serious known defects and is being sold as is. There is little point in illustrating the multiple deficiencies of a home as a seller in an inspection report when you know the buyer will probably be ordering their own inspection.
- If you are asking a high price for the home and sticking to it. You know the buyer will be getting an inspection but you have already decided not to negotiate.
- You think the home may have a high level of radon. If your home is found to have a high level of radon (see chapter ten), and you decide to not install a ventilation system to lower it, the buyer may ask you to install one. This is expected and reasonable, but radon mitigation systems are not inexpensive. I personally think you would want to know the radon level, but it's your choice.

Other advantages to seller ordered inspections include:

- The seller knows the home. The home inspector will be able to get answers to his/her questions on the history of any problems they find.

- 🔍 A home inspection will help the seller be more objective when it comes to setting a fair price on the home.
- 🔍 The seller will be alerted to any safety issues found in the home before they open it up for tours.

Most home inspectors offer substantial discounts for seller inspections, and it is typical for the inspection to also include a return follow-up with an updated report. Getting a seller's home inspection gives you a substantial advantage in selling your home for the best price, and usually reduces the amount of stress that selling a home induces. You will have all of the knowledge without any of the surprises.

"A home should be a stockade, a refuge from the flaming arrows of anxiety, tension and worry." ~ Wilfred Peterson

Chapter 3: What Owners Need to Know

You've moved in. The inspection report did not turn up any surprises. What now? Put the report into the file folder Home Sale Docs and load the box into a corner of the basement closet. Or not?

Not. If you file the report away now, you're missing an opportunity to once again head off wallet-busting surprises. Keep the report out and file the rest of the information in a safe place.

Go through the report and highlight any information having to do with component life and component condition. For example, if your inspector tells you that your water heater is in good condition and you know it is eight years old, you can find out how many years this type of water heater will last. You will then be able to budget for its replacement. Unless your home is brand new (we'll get to that), you will be able to identify the approximate replacement cycles for your heating, ventilation, and cooling (HVAC) equipment, water heater, washer and dryer, refrigerators, decking, roofing, and more.

This step is time consuming, but once you've done it, you'll be able to budget future expenses in the home. Instead of hearing the cry, "Honey, there's no hot water," you'll be able to identify the approximate point of failure and have a plan ready. Most appliances display warning signals of impending failure, even hot water heaters.

Set up a notebook or binder, and name it something like Home Components Service Life and Maintenance. List out the appliances and components. List their condition, and add a date for replacement. The equipment will likely survive longer than this marker in the calendar, but at least you won't be surprised, and you will have the item in the budget. It's always a welcome situation to have an appliance last much longer than you thought it would. Refrigerators and laundry equipment often surprise us this way.

You might be thinking, *I have no clue as to what dates to put here*. That's okay. Believe it or not, if you call your inspector and ask for some help on this, they'll usually be happy to go through the report with you and help you identify these items and dates. Offer to pay them to review it, but expect that most will do this as a part of the review in your recent inspection.

The life of appliances, roofing, electronics, and materials in a home can be found online by typing in "home components life expectancy." A free chart is also available from the International Association of Certified Home Inspectors as a downloadable pdf.[1]

Regular maintenance will affect these dates positively. If you really want to save money, combine routine recommended maintenance with inspections and replacement planning. Cold water and financial surprises will be rare.

If you want to get even more ambitious and organized, add service records, serial numbers, maintenance schedules, and other relevant information to your notebook. I like to leave the service manual with the appliance, but I also make a photocopy of the specifications and maintenance intervals for the notebook. You'll find a remarkable amount of time savings when you have the specifications at hand, whether it's spark plugs for the tractor or air filter sizes for the HVAC.

---

[1] https://inspectoroutlet.com/products/life-expectancy-chart

One proactive thing you can do when you get your home inspection is to ask the inspector for their opinion on each appliance's condition. Tell them that you're assembling the information so you can head off surprises. The inspector will have a newfound respect for you as a homeowner, and even though they say, "I can't predict anything for you," they might share opinions face to face.

Asking your inspector to recommend maintenance companies and repair contractors is likely a dead end. This is because they don't want to get involved in making a recommendation and having it either look like a conflict of interest or having it come back to bite them in some form. But ask anyway. For current issue repairs, they may be able to tell you who they like. I have found that if the contractor information is not current, you can risk having a disappointing experience. This is because the reliability and competence of many repair companies changes month to month.

Consider getting another home inspection five years after moving into your home. Get the same inspector if you can, and ask for a discount. They will remember you (yes, we inspectors remember every home we've ever inspected. It's a strange blessing or curse, I'm not sure which), and they will instinctively give you a discount because they know you, and the pressure is less than inspecting a home under contract.

This reinspection every five years will help you identify what you're missing in your own attention to detail. It's well worth the cost.

If you decide to sell your home, you will have an impressive array of maintenance and component information for the next owner. This signals quality and attention to detail to most buyers.

"Help others achieve their dreams and you will achieve yours." ~ Les Brown

Chapter 4: What Agents Need to Know

If you've been in real estate for any length of time, you know about home inspections. Along with the other due diligence tasks you oversee, you know home inspections can be fraught with drama, disagreements, and misunderstandings. This is the real world of selling real estate, and it will test your patience and experience. I'm going to offer some advice that should be helpful even to the agents who have been around the block.

We begin with the regulations, which are fairly consistent state to state. As I read through the advice that state boards or commissions offer on home inspections, one, in particular, stands out for its clarity:

> Brokers who represent prospective buyers and tenants should advise and encourage their clients to order inspections, tests and surveys for properties they wish to buy or lease and may furnish them with lists of licensed, competent service providers to contact and hire.
>
> A broker should never discourage a client from ordering an inspection, test or survey, even if it is not required. Inspections are an extremely important part of the purchase process for every buyer and in some commercial leasing transactions for tenants. Moreover, a prospective buyer's refusal to order an inspection in an effort to save money may have dire consequences in the long run.[2]

This advice makes sense, and most agents don't have any issues with it. Where things get thorny are in two areas. The first is how you

---

[2] Fussell, Stephen L., 2016. "Handling Inspections: Guidelines for Brokers." *North Carolina Real Estate Commission Real Estate Bulletin* 2016-V46-3, p.4.
http://www.ncrec.gov/Pdfs/Bulletins/Feb2016-Vol46-3.pdf

choose and recommend inspectors to clients, and the second is how inspectors handle the reporting and communications with clients.

Choosing and Recommending Home Inspectors

Home inspectors want to develop a relationship with real estate offices because the offices can provide a steady stream of work. Be choosy. Once you've done your due diligence choosing an inspector, they can make your business more efficient, reliable, and professional.

Interview inspectors before handing their cards and brochures out to clients. You are already good at judging people or you wouldn't be in the real estate business. Spend enough time with an inspector to feel confident in your recommendation.

Your questions should include what certification and licensing they have, and how many years they've been inspecting. You're not hiring this person to work directly for you, but if you recommend them to a client, you'd like them to display your own level of professionalism. Home inspectors must be thoroughly honest and operate with the highest of ethical standards, just as you do. Inspectors spend hours by themselves in client homes, and so their integrity must be above reproach.

As you evaluate inspectors, pay attention to their professional appearance and the vehicle they drive. You already know these characteristics speak volumes to your clients and reflect your own professional attitudes and brand.

If things do not go well in the interview with an inspector, realize that this is as good as it gets. Whatever problems you discover in the interview are not likely to go away.

Even a qualified and experienced inspector can wreak havoc for everyone if they have a habit of lumping minor issues in with truly serious problems in a report. How your inspector positions and communicates these issues is critical. You can ask them how they handle minor versus serious issues. You should also ask them for a sample report.

Give your clients the ability to choose. Also, tell them that they can choose an inspector who is not on your list. Your client may or may not want to do the research on an inspector, but they will appreciate you giving them the option.

Since real estate professionals are vested in the sale financially, should they be recommending home inspectors with whom they have a working relationship? As long as the client is comfortable choosing an inspector this way—where the client is provided options—and clearly knows that they can search out their own inspector, my opinion is that it is not a conflict of interest. Agents understand that a home with under-reported defects can be a time bomb waiting to go off.

Reporting and Communications
Home inspection reports across the United States have become highly standardized because of the rules and regulations surrounding home inspections. The formatting is helpful, but the amount of detail can be intimidating to your client. Ask to see a sample report, and confirm that it's clear and professional.

While the findings in the report can be straightforward, the presentation of the findings can be troublesome. From my years as an inspector, I can tell you that some of the problems I found in homes caused me to make a bigger deal out of them than I should have. Sometimes called the *picky inspector syndrome*, inexperience is usually at the core of this bad habit. New inspectors are terrified they will miss something important.

When the inspector is discussing the issues with you it's one thing; when they are discussing the issues with the client, it's another. After a few inspections, you will discover how these communications go with your client. What inspectors say to the client, the seller, if they are present, and to any other agents at the property do carry substantial weight, so it requires restraint and composure.

Many inspectors are introverts. This may make them more nervous in their communications. What you hope for is to find a technically experienced and competent inspector who is also good at communicating with your clients in a logical and balanced way. This balance may be the most critical skill you evaluate as you consider which inspectors to put on your list.

The inspectors you choose should be highly experienced. It's not that a new inspector will miss things, it's that a new inspector may have trouble differentiating between what is serious and what is not.

By all means, give a newbie a chance, but realize you may spend more time helping your buyer understand the importance of the defects. A deck that has to be rebuilt (serious) and a stair rail code deviation (not serious) are two very different things. Years of experience improve an inspector's ability to sniff out real trouble and reduce the drama around lesser items. Experience provides the balance you and your client need.

When do you need specialists? Since home inspectors are generalists, they are not in a position to grade the seriousness of a defect or assess the cost of repair for serious defects. They will suggest a review by a specialist in these cases.

There is no obligation to get a specialist, but it's a good idea if any item needs a technical analysis. It is the major defects that can cause major expenses after the buyer is in the home, and evaluating them is the whole point of getting the home inspected.

The bottom line is being able to choose inspectors who can differentiate between serious structural flaws and less serious deviations. The moniker "picky" is not assigned because inspectors are too thorough, but that they are not adequately distinguishing between what is serious and what is minor.

A Few More Tips
There is so much boilerplate in inspection reports that you'll think the report was written in advance. This is annoying, but unless you think the inspector actually skipped inspection areas, it's a given.

Depending on what area of the country your business is in, you'll see the same safety items over and over. These typically involve items that are not to code (missing plumbing vents under sinks, distance on railing verticals, structural defects on decks, and lint buildup in dryer vents). Rely on the inspector to put these in perspective for you and the buyer. They should flag anything that is a serious safety issue.

Encourage the buyer to attend the inspection. The communication of flaws in a home always goes better face-to-face. Inspectors prefer to show up early and inspect as much as possible alone. This allows them to concentrate. You and the buyer can show up near the end of the inspection and do a walk-through.

If it's not possible for the buyer to attend the inspection, encourage them to call the inspector for a recap. Inspectors aren't excited about phone calls because they can be time consuming but for the buyer, it's more direct than simply reading the report, and allows for the inspector to communicate nuances about the home that might not get into the report.

It's always better for the seller to leave the home during the inspection. It provides for more concentration and fewer awkward moments.

Remember that home inspectors are not specialists. They should not be estimating repair costs or recommending contractors, however honest and innocent it appears. This goes against what I told buyers in the first chapter—they should try asking for referrals face to face—they might get some goods answers. However, it's still the norm to get the response, "I cannot refer others."

We've spent most of this chapter talking about buyer inspections. Remember that sellers can benefit from getting an inspection in advance of the listing, or shortly thereafter. Seller inspections often cost less, with a promise to return and reinspect, and an updated report to show off to interested buyers. See Chapter 2:

What Sellers Need to Know. It's better to identify the surprises in advance than have them jump out at you.

"Errors like straws upon the surface flow, Who would search for pearls to be grateful for often must dive below." ~ John Dryden

Chapter 5: What Builders Need to Know

There's nothing quite so exciting as designing and building your own custom home. Most people who take this route to their dream are delighted and say they would do it again. But these same people, in a confidential interview, said they encountered a host of problems having a custom home built. From construction delays and cost overruns to discovering structural faults, they were confronted with enough issues to consider quitting the project or selling the home soon after moving in. What's going on here?

Everyone makes mistakes. From designers and architects to builders and owners, it's normal and natural to miss things. The key is catching the mistakes before the home is finished.

Those of you who have had homes built might recall finding issues with the home after moving in. A builder will tell you that this is completely normal; there is no way that they could have identified and corrected everything in the home, given the complexity of the systems. "It goes with the territory," one builder told me.

Home builders try very hard to build the best house for you and not make mistakes. But builders are busy, and managing subcontractors is not an easy process. The superintendent can't be at your house all the time overseeing the work.

Although the issues can be minor—the cold-water faucet runs hot, a light switch does not work, a window is stuck, a threshold seal is missing, door hardware is loose—the problems list can be the tip of a glacier where you do not see the bigger issues hidden below the surface.

The big issues can include ungrounded electrical outlets, plumbing pipe unions installed upside down, heating and air conditioning ductwork hooked up to the wrong zones or cross-connected, missing return air ducts, undersized electrical circuits, oversized air compressors, and incorrect or missing weight-bearing structure. As a contractor and former home inspector, I have personally seen all of these and more. Here's a story.

A snowstorm raged outside as I drove into the garage for the first time. The truck was covered in a tall layer of snow. I got out and closed the truck cab door and a big chunk of snow fell to the floor. I assumed the melting snow would run off to the front of the two-car garage where we'd asked the contractor to install a drain. Excited and delighted to be in a newly constructed home and exhausted from a long day, I went upstairs and fell into bed.

The next morning, I walked down the stairs to the basement to find two inches of standing water throughout the garage and first floor rooms, soaking the new carpet, baseboards, and wood flooring. I was aghast. Then in shock, I got it. *The water is running the wrong way.*

The concrete contractor had poured the entire slab for the house with the wrong slope. Instead of three degrees sloping to the outside, as it should have been, it was three degrees sloping to the inside. Drains won't help if the water can't reach them.

In a panic, I located the shop vac and began vacuuming water. Gallons and gallons of water.

There is little to be done to correct a situation like this except park outside in storms or have a large shop vac handy. This could have been prevented with a thorough inspection and a checklist. Whose fault was it? Mine. I didn't inspect for it and should have. When I was visiting the jobsite during the build and noticed rainwater collecting toward the inside back of the basement, I should have realized the error. It was a half-formed nagging thought at the time. I should have been more attentive.

As experienced and competent as our city building inspectors are, they only look at very specific construction items. Building inspectors pay attention to building code items, which are designed to keep us safe. They are likely to miss patio and garage drainage slopes because they are not looking for it, nor is it on their checklist.

So . . . what do you do?

You have two choices. The first is to leave it up to the builder and hope that they will catch the errors. Or you can hire a licensed home inspector to perform multiple inspections during the course of the build. At a minimum, I recommend an inspection prior to foundation pour, prior to drywall, and an inspection just before your walk-through with the builder. The inspector's list will carry over to your own punch list.

I also recommend that you hire a structural building engineer and have them perform an inspection just before concrete is poured and before drywall.

Both professionals will provide you with a list of issues. It's your money and your contract, so the builder should be pleased that you provided the punch list detail. It makes their job easier since they are doing their best to identify all the issues themselves.

However—there are builders who will not allow independent inspections. They think it is a criticism of their expertise if an inspector finds something wrong. My advice is to find a different builder.

The more eyes you get on the project, the better. Would you rather spend a couple thousand dollars while the home is being built (less than one percent of the average custom-built home price of $350K-$600K) or wait with fingers crossed that all will be perfect? Based upon what I've discovered with home inspections, the extra money spent will pay dividends.

Let me repeat that. *Based upon what I've discovered with home inspections, the extra money spent on independent inspections will pay dividends.*

Building Contracts

Put a clause in your building contract that permits you to hire independent inspectors. Add that the builder will agree to review the inspection recommendations and correct errors that they are responsible for at their expense.

Make a list of the items in your builder's contract that say *variable* or *depends on*. These are items that are not fixed in a fixed-cost contract. These are the surprise areas. Any builder who has started a custom home knows that not everything can be predicted—from weather conditions holding up the schedule and/or damaging work already done—to unintentional errors caused by subcontractors. Typical areas that cause overruns include excavation, footings, and plan errors. Ask your builder to help you calculate what these things could cost worst-case and be ready. If things go well, you will be delighted.

Double-check the materials list. Are you completely sure you picked out all the right fixtures and appliances? Lighting? Where wall switches go? Review these in detail. If you have gotten so close to the plans and lists that you're not objective, ask someone else to look at it with you. When you move into the house and realize that the bathroom fixtures are not the ones you chose, it will not be the builder's responsibility. How do you think I found that out?

Keep a list of action items for the builder. They will appreciate the attention you are paying to your home; it makes their job much easier to have an informed owner. Many successful builders have dozens of homes underway at any given time with a limited number of superintendents. They may not get to the project every day. Ask them what format and what frequency they prefer for the issues list.

Builders will warranty your home for a year. Many owners simply move in and forget about the warranty unless something obvious goes wrong. This is a mistake. You should keep a detailed list of issues you find—and you will find them—and you should email them to the builder. This helps the builder on scheduling. Items can include loose toilet tanks, grout cracking, nail pops in drywall, vinyl floors lifting, windows that are stuck, places they forgot to caulk, adjusting the heating and cooling vents for balance, etc.

When you take the time to actively manage your custom home project along with the builder and the added independent inspections, you will save yourself from the typical financial shocks and end up with a much higher quality home.

Who is Doing the Building?
Are you doing the building? If you're constructing your own home or acting as your own contractor, it's even more critical to have an independent inspector helping you.

Arrange to meet with your home inspector well in advance of your construction start. Review plans, and ask them what inspections they think should be made in-process.

Attend the inspections. Make a list of what they find. Even the most conscientious subcontractors are going to miss things. Who ends up paying for mistakes? You do, unless you catch it close to the time it happens and notify the subcontractor. If you forgo these inspections because you are busy, or don't want to pay someone to help you, you are likely to pay another 15–20 percent for the home or live with mistakes that can't be corrected later.

Special Attention Items
Your builder will be as efficient as they can be so they don't have to overspend on your project. I've found a few areas where they want you to believe items are "extra" when in fact they should be standard. Review your contract thoroughly. Two common items that get overlooked are the Energy Recovery System (ERV) that provides air exchange in the home, and ventilation to the outside for gas and cooking appliances.

According to the Environmental Protection Agency (EPA), indoor air is far more polluted than outside air, even in rural areas. This is because all of the activities that we humans do—from cooking to breathing—contribute to poor air quality in a concentrated environment.

The EPA recommends an air exchange rate of at least 0.35 air changes per hour but not less than 15 cubic feet of air per minute (cfm) per person in residential buildings to minimize adverse health effects.

I inspected a recently constructed home for a client and noticed that there was no air exchanger (ERV) in the home. I asked the builder why. His answer was, "It's another thousand dollars and the owner didn't ask for it." Bad answer! With modern construction as tight as it is, leaving out the air exchanger is an invitation to condensation and poor indoor air quality.

Some states require a Blower Door Test before a home can get its Certificate of Occupancy (CO). This test is simple and measures how airtight the home is—a measure of efficiency. But curiously, there is no requirement for an air exchanger (ERV or HRV).

Make sure you have all gas appliances fully vented to the outside. Cooking and indoor fireplaces contribute heavily to inside air pollution. Putting in air vents is extra work for builders so you should make sure the contract stipulates the types and numbers of vents in the home. Vents for cooking and gas appliances should exit to the outside, not the inside.

"Nature will bear the closest inspection. She invites us to lay our eye level with her smallest leaf, and take an insect view of its plain."
~ Henry David Thoreau

Chapter 6: Choosing an Inspector

We love what we do. Every inspection is an adventure with mysteries to solve. We love every part of it, including the hard-to-see places—because that is where no one else is looking. The tougher it is, the more we revel in our ability to find what's wrong and what's right.

Although we enjoy good homes with few problems, we get a thrill when we find a serious problem that would have bitten the next owner. We like to think we are saving people both trauma and money.

Our first challenge is actually finding a property. I have ended up in quarries following the

GPS and in narrow no-turn-around roads leading to mountaintops, dense forests, and valley creek fording trails. I've been in cities with buildings so tall the GPS couldn't get a fix.

We enjoy interpreting problems for our customers and doing the briefing. We have a sense of satisfaction when we assemble a report and get it to the customer.

It's a physically demanding job. We carry heavy ladders, squeeze through small openings into the unknown, and walk four miles on a typical inspection. We contend with wild dogs, bear, foxes, rats, rabbits, skunks, raccoons, spiders, and snakes. Sometimes we have to hike into a property when we don't have the gate key. We work in every kind of weather. We carry a large kit of tools and instruments, the most important being our cameras and our binoculars.

Training is thorough. After a week-long class with both theory and hands-on, the day ends with real home inspections. I spent six months as an apprentice to another inspector before I became a solo inspector. I passed three exams and have recurrent training every year.

What are Home Inspectors?
There is confusion about what home inspectors can and cannot do, and what their mission is. They are often mistaken for building inspectors,

pest inspectors, and appraisers. Let's clear up the confusion.

A municipal or city building inspector reviews permits, zoning, set-back requirements, and code compliance for a property. Some municipalities require this review before a sale.

If you are building a new home, it will be inspected at intervals by a building inspector who will make sure the home meets building codes and other city requirements.

A home inspector, on the other hand, does not work for the city and is independently licensed by the state (if the state requires licensing). There is no requirement in any state to have a home inspection report if you are buying a home.

A home inspector covers a much broader range of issues in a home than building code inspectors and appraisers. As generalists, home inspectors possess experience in construction, building materials, home design, electrical design, plumbing, and heating and air-conditioning. They know building codes, the life expectancy of components, deck systems, and safety practices. While they could probably change out a water heater or build you a deck, what they specialize in is *inspection*. They are really good at catching what's wrong and explaining it.

A home inspector is not a general contractor and vice versa, although many contractors are also home inspectors.

Home inspectors do not check zoning compliance, permits, setback requirements, homeowner association requirements, or test fire sprinklers.

There is also confusion between home *inspectors* and home *appraisers*. Appraisers collect information about the home and analyze data to arrive at a market value for the property. The information they collect includes square footage, prices of surrounding homes, and previous sales price data. The report they produce reflects their judgment and opinion based on the data.

Appraisers are typically hired by the lending institution, and the buyer pays for the report. They may or may not actually enter the home if they have recent data and photographs.

How to Choose a Home Inspector
Professional qualifications. Your inspector should be credentialed by a major home inspection organization. The best known is the American Society of Home Inspectors (ASHI), and the International Association of Certified Home Inspectors (InterNACHI). Requirements for membership are strict and the organizations provide ongoing education. Your inspector may also be state-licensed. As of 2021, thirty-five

states in the U.S. require home inspectors to be licensed.

Experience. We all had to start somewhere. In the first few years of my own home inspection career, I made plenty of mistakes, missed things I should have seen, and called out things I should not have worried about. Learn from me; employ a home inspector with at least two years of experience. Over five years is even better. You are going to pay the same amount of money either way. Experience is the single most important qualification a credentialed inspector can have.

Many states with licensing requirements also require yearly recurrent training. This is a bonus, as it keeps inspectors up to date.

Detailed reporting. Ask your prospective inspectors for a link to a sample report. The inspection report detail is important and can run more than twenty pages. More is better. Look for easy-to-read copy with trouble areas broken out with explanations. The inspector will email you a pdf version or direct you to their website.

Reputation. Social media may be helpful in finding out what experiences other clients have had with a given inspector. While you don't want a "picky" inspector, you do want a "thorough" inspector. Your real estate agent can be helpful on this point since they deal with inspectors on a constant basis.

Agents will not suffer an inspector that spends time picking out small details and does not elevate the serious items. Nor do they choose the "easiest" inspectors to make a sale. Agents want you to be happy in your new home, and they have their own reputations to protect.

Cost. Don't haggle over the price. In any given geographical area, inspections will cost about the same. The money you spend on a home inspection will pay for itself in maintenance knowledge, resale potential, and heading off any major expenses.

Discounts. Although I just said not to haggle, a polite request for a discount can't hurt. The worst thing that can happen will be that the inspector will say no. Sometimes they will say yes.

Agreement. Make sure your inspector gives you a detailed agreement ahead of the inspection. Read the detail. It's your only course of action if there's a problem. Make sure you understand that your inspector can't see through walls and doesn't inspect for termites.

Advanced tools. Ask your inspector how they will inspect the roof and crawlspace. They should answer visual inspection and cameras. Advanced tools may be a plus for areas that are tough to get to, but are not required.

Drones are especially useful for the roof and remote-control robots for the crawlspace. They can both be controlled with a smartphone and provide a clear video feed. I wish I'd had them when I was inspecting.

Website. Professional home inspectors will have professional websites. You may find everything you need to know on the site, including a sample report and links to social media. It's likely you will also be directed to the website for report pickup. This is a great system because it's fast and easy.

Social Media. It's likely your inspector will have a Facebook page and other media-sharing sites. Look on their website for the icons and links. Read what people have to say. When I was inspecting, I enjoyed posting anonymous pictures of serious defects so folks could get a sense for what we do. From the opaque with mold swimming pool to the structural joists cut out to move a wall, I got lots of traffic.

"Errors accumulate in the sketch and compound in the model." ~ Leon Battista Alberti

Chapter 7: Top Five Inspection Myths

A home inspection covers everything.
Myth. A home inspector will spend hours on an inspection, but there's a lot that they can't see. They can't determine if there's a problem inside the walls, they can't move furniture to see something, and they can't determine if there will be a failure right after the buyers move in.

Most home inspectors are not licensed to perform specialist inspections. These inspections include termite and other insect infestations, mold identification, pool and spa inspections, and well and septic inspections.

Home inspectors will give you a heads up on anything they find concerning so you can get the right professional to evaluate it.

The inspector will find your presence at the inspection disturbing.
Myth. While it is true that home inspectors are a somewhat introverted, geeky bunch of guys and gals that secretly say they would rather be alone, the truth is that misunderstandings and communication errors will be greatly reduced if you attend the inspection. Attending the inspection will also allow you to get good advice on the home's systems. Inspectors will be able to convey far more information to you in person than you can get out of the report, no matter how detailed it is. The best of both worlds will be showing up at the end of the inspection and getting a briefing.

There is no point in a seller getting their own inspection since the buyer is going to get one.
Myth. Sellers in particular can benefit from getting a home inspection *before* listing the home. Waiting and depending on the buyers to alert you to faults puts you behind the curve. See Chapter 2: What Sellers Need to Know.

A brand-new home or a freshly restored home does not need a home inspection before you buy it.
Myth. All homes, whether they are one-month-old, one-hundred-years-old, or just came out of a makeover, will benefit from an inspection. New and custom-built homes in particular have a slate of mistakes and oversights that need to be caught and remedied before you move in.

At the end of the inspection, the inspector will score your home on quality and advise you on whether you should buy or not.
Myth. Of course, anyone would want this. While the report you receive will be very thorough, it will not score the home in any way. The inspector will not advise you on whether you should buy the home or not. There are several reasons for this. The first is that the inspector is only looking at what is visible and accessible. The second is that the inspector, as a generalist, is not going to grade every system and appliance in the home.

This is just one reason for you to attend the inspection personally. You will be able to gain a great deal from listening to the inspector. While inspectors try their best to be completely objective as they talk to you about the home, you will get a much better "feel" for the home than you would by just reading the written report.

"It is not the beauty of a building you should look at; it's the construction of the foundation that will stand the test of time."
~ David Allan Coe

Chapter 8: How to Use the Report

I'm an airplane nut. Several summers ago at an airshow, I gave a talk about building your own airplane. After the talk, someone came up to me and said they were going to purchase a used experimental aircraft that very day. I asked them who they were having inspect the craft before the purchase? They said that they were skipping the inspection, saying, "It flew in here to the show so it must be fine."

If you're buying a house, this is like saying the home's roof doesn't leak water so everything else must be fine inside.

Whether you are buying an airplane or a home, get an inspection. The price you pay will pale in comparison to what you might end up spending to correct major defects. Here's how to use an inspection report to save you money.

Don't worry about the small stuff. A stuck window can be fixed. A leaky faucet can be repaired. Missing attic insulation can be added. You can even ask the seller to make repairs. They don't have to, but many times they will to make you happy. Skip over these items in the report and go to the section called Major Items. Usually, these are at the top of the list in the report and/or in the summary.

In most states, the seller is supposed to tell you about significant defects in the home (called a "material defect disclosure"). This rarely happens. This is not necessarily because the seller is covering it up, but because they don't know about it. I have gone into dozens of basements to find furnaces that were recalled because of carbon monoxide hazards and the owner had no idea (and was lucky). Carbon monoxide leaking into a home can be fatal.

The significant items that you want to focus on are the things that will either hit your wallet in a big way or will be a risk to your safety and well-being in the home. The maintenance and repair items are handy to have, but every home has them.

A few final points. The first is that there is no requirement to do anything with a home inspection report. The report contains the advice of a qualified and experienced inspector so that the seller and buyer can determine the condition of the home and head off unanticipated surprises. The second point is to rely on your real estate agent for perspective. They have done this many times, and as a professional will give you accurate and thoughtful advice.

"I should say: the house shelters day-dreaming, the house protects the dreamer, the house allows one to dream in peace."
~ Gaston Bachelard

Chapter 9: Additional Inspections

Because your home inspector is a generalist, they will recommend a specialist if they see something that concerns them. For example, if they think the plumbing is slow running, they may say you should get a septic or sewer inspection.

Make a list of these recommendations. While you do not have to engage any of the specialists, it may save you money over the long run.

I'll list the most common specialty tests and inspections and tell you whether your inspector can do them. I'll also render an opinion on how important it is to get a particular inspection.

Listen carefully to your inspector's advice. They are making recommendations based on years of experience.

Termite and pest infestations. Your inspector is usually not licensed to perform a Wood Destroying Organism (WDO) inspection. Get a pest professional. Highly recommended for every home inspection. Termite damage can be hidden in walls and foundations and cause severe structural damage.

Radon. Can be conducted by home inspectors. If you are buying or building in an area of the country where radon is common, then you definitely want this inspection. See the next chapter to learn about radon. You can buy a kit and do this test yourself for less than fifty dollars.

Water. Can be conducted by home inspectors but the sample is sent to a water testing lab or taken to the local health department for testing. Recommended if the home is on well water. Basic tests are inexpensive and take several days; a full chemical analysis panel is expensive and can take weeks. You can also do the test yourself by taking a water sample and sending it to a lab. Well drilling companies can perform the testing and they also send the sample out to a lab. You should at least get a bacterial contamination test, which is included in the basic tests and is not expensive. This tests for E. coli and coliform bacteria in your water. No level of fecal matter is acceptable in a water sample.

Septic or Sewer. Not conducted by home inspectors. Not recommended unless there appears to be a problem. Septic systems should be inspected every three to five years.

Alarm Systems. Not conducted by home inspectors. If the alarm is professionally monitored, the company can do the inspection. There may or may not be a fee.

Lawn Sprinklers. May or may not be included in a home inspection. Plumbers can inspect and repair.

Indoor Air Quality. Not recommended unless there is some reason for concern, such as finding mold. Ask your home inspector for a referral. The Environmental Protection Agency (EPA.gov) also has information on indoor air quality on its website.

Mold. Not recommended unless the home inspector has a concern. Molds can cause allergic reactions such as upper respiratory symptoms including coughing, sneezing, wheezing, runny nose, and shortness of breath. You can find an inspector by going to the National Organization of Remediators and Mold Inspectors.

A mold inspection employs surface and air sampling to determine the type of mold and tests for humidity levels and water intrusion. Inspectors use thermal imaging devices to find damp or cold spots behind walls and recommend how to remove them.

Mold inspectors should be certified by the Institute of Inspection Certification and Restoration Certification (IICRC).

Structural Inspection. Not recommended unless the home inspector has a concern. They will refer you to a licensed engineer if they flag something.

Chimney. The home inspector will inspect the firebox visually and the chimney components from the attic and the roof as a part of your inspection. If they find cracked mortar, creosote build-up (byproduct of burning wood), or flue defects, they will recommend a chimney sweep. Fires that begin in the flue can burn the entire house down quickly.

Pools and spas. Recommended if your home includes a pool and/or spa. Your home inspector will not conduct these specialized inspections but can refer you to a testing company.

Contaminants. Lead (in paint), asbestos (in insulation), and other contaminants may be found in homes constructed before 1978. If you are concerned, ask your inspector for a referral to a risk assessor. Visit EPA.gov.

"Home, the spot of earth supremely blest, A dearer, sweeter spot than all the rest."
~ Robert Montgomery

Chapter 10: Radon Facts

Since talking about a colorless, odorless, radioactive gas can be boring, I've assembled a quiz to make it more interesting. If you know all about radon already, then you can ace the quiz.

Why should you care? Because radon, a gas, can be found inside homes in varying amounts. If the concentrations are high, radon contributes to lung cancer second only behind smoking cigarettes.

Radon gas comes from outer space during the daytime and is similar to the radiation from the sun. True or False?
False. Radon comes from the natural radioactive breakdown of uranium in soil, rock, and water,

and ends up in the air we breathe. Radon is colorless, odorless, and tasteless. Radon can also be found in water.

Testing for radon is complicated and time consuming and you need a professional to perform the test. True or False?
False. You can buy a test kit at your local home improvement store for less than fifty dollars. The test takes a few days—you simply hang the kit in your home and then send it to a lab. Sometimes you can get a test kit free at local county or city health departments.

Radon levels averaging over 4.0 pCi/L are considered unsafe. True or False?
True. Radon in the air is measured in picocuries per liter of air, or pCi/L. Levels less than 4 pCi/L are considered safe, although many experts are advising 2.0 pCi/L or less is much better.

Exposure to high levels of radon causes twice as many deaths every year as drunk driving in the United States. True or False?
True. Radon causes over twenty thousand deaths a year from lung cancer, while drunk driving causes over ten thousand fatalities a year (EPA.gov).

The top floor of your home will test the highest for radon because the gas rises. True or False?
False. Radon seeps into the lowest level of your home from the ground, and barriers such as plastic, insulation, and flooring slow it down. Sometimes simply sealing foundation cracks and slab cracks and fixing air leaks will lower radon to safer levels.

The amount of radon in the air outside your home is zero. True or False?
False. The average outside level is actually .4 pCi/L, or picocuries per liter (EPA.gov).

Radon levels vary in level from state to state and can be high in the mountain areas. True or False?
True. Although radon levels vary throughout the United States, radon has been found in every state. I have inspected homes in the mountains of North Carolina that registered over 35 pCi/L. Yes, you read that right—thirty-five—over eight times an acceptable level.

If you test your home for radon and find levels exceeding what is considered safe, you will have to move out and have the building remediated. True or False?
False. This is the good news—if you need to reduce the levels of radon in your home, it is not

overly expensive to do. A vent and fan system is usually the first line of defense and will lower the radon to acceptable levels over 75 percent of the time.

Can you ask a seller to remediate their home if high levels are found? Yes, you can. In fact, you should ask—at the worst you will be able to get a discount on the selling price and then you can have the remediation performed before you move in.

How did you do? Learn more by going to the Environmental Protection Agency's website www.epa.gov and www.radon.com.

"True stories are always good because they're so odd, and so unlikely."
~ Steven Knight

Chapter 11: True Stories

Home inspectors as a group have an amazing array of stories. They range from scary to creepy to heart-warming. The most fun I have is going to recurrent training with other inspectors and meeting in the bar at the end of the day. We never run out of stories.

They range from hydraulic car jacks holding up floor beams and doorways to basements with missing stairs to fuse panels with pennies installed and jewelry heaped into HVAC ducts.

Crawlspaces
I suit up in head-to-toe Tyvek coveralls when I crawl into the spaces underneath a home. Even the tiniest of crawlspaces yield critical clues

about the condition of the home. It is also one of the most dangerous places you can go. From brown recluse spiders to hibernating bears, to a variety of poisonous snakes, it must be navigated with great care and constant attention.

In addition to the Tyvek suit I wear an airtight mask with breathing filters and a Plexiglas face shield to protect against a variety of molds, bacteria, viruses, and spores. Sometimes I feel like the guy in the spacesuit in the movie *Alien*.

One day I was inspecting a large cabin in the mountains. The cabin was in a remote area, with a seven-mile-long unimproved and narrow gravel road leading to it.

Winding up through the dense forest and passing the five-thousand-foot altitude on my GPS, I pondered why people would want to be this remote.

The answer came to me as I pulled up to the sprawling vacant cabin. Set in against the deep woods, the view from the front porch was one of delicately pastel-shadowed mountain ranges stretching out to the horizon in a multi-colored panorama. I stood quietly on the deck drinking in the stunning beauty of the early morning scene.

A roughly mown lawn met a garden of native perennials with blue and gold lantana and daisies.

But no one is living here. I wondered why it had received the recent care. I abandoned my ponderings and got to work, strapping on my inspector's belt with everything from screwdrivers to cameras to bear spray.

After walking the roof and inspecting the inside rooms, I hunted for the outside entry to the crawlspace. In the back of the cabin, I found it facing the woods. The door was fastened shut with a padlock and hasp, hanging unlocked.

Good.

The opening, however, was really small. Not unusual. I wondered how the bigger inspectors got through these doors. I was all of five foot seven inches tall and a hundred and eighteen pounds, so I could get through these spaces.

They don't go in.

I removed the padlock from the hasp and opened the door. Darkness.

I wriggled through the twenty-inch square opening and onto the dirt floor. I held up the flashlight. In the arc of yellow light floated dust particles and whispery cobweb threads. Large wolf spiders stood their ground in the spaces between the beams only inches above my head. I noted the fallen insulation to my left, where I knew snakes like to sleep. The stillness was only broken by the sound of dripping water in the distance.

Crawling slowly on my belly, I quietly passed the insulation pile and headed for the black pool of water at the far end. I crawled past fallen insulation squares, mouse carcasses, and pieces of plastic sheeting. Out of the corner of my eye, I caught movement to my right. Rotating my light beam, I was startled to see three pairs of reflective yellow circles move and then stop. Raccoons. I heard a chittering, snarling, sound.

I noticed the yellow cast of my flashlight beginning to falter. Then I heard the tiny door behind me slam shut and the scraping metal of the padlock clasp closing.

Trapped.

An icy wave washed over my body from head to foot as I tried to understand what was happening. I felt the ceiling beams closing down on me. Such a tight space.

Get out! I felt out of breath.

Instinctively I began shouting at the top of my lungs. "Hey! Hey!" I turned around and started crawling and sliding toward the little door.

I gave a wide berth to the pile of insulation, hoping I hadn't woken up the sleeping snakes. I reached the door and used the back end of the heavy light to bang on it. My heart was racing and I willed it to slow and come up with a plan to escape.

I heard a man's voice.

"Hey, what? Is there someone in there?"

"Yes, the home inspector! Please open the door."

"Okay, okay, hold on. My goodness."

I heard metal on rasp, and the door popped open.

I flew through that opening so fast I startled the man, who backed up several steps, tripped over a branch on the ground and fell into a pile of leaves. He was shaking his head.

"You look like an astronaut," he blurted out.

I removed my headgear and took some deep breaths, realizing I now understood what claustrophobia was.

The man stared at me. "Gosh, I'm sorry. I didn't know you were in there. I'm the yard guy and I saw the door was open to the crawl. Don't want any animals in there, right?" He laughed nervously.

"Of course, but you sure did give me a scare," I said. "I wasn't expecting anyone to be here."

"Sorry about that. If I'd know I would have left the hatch open."

"All's well that ends well."

I decided that the crawlspace inspection was finished. My photos would show the leak over the black pool.

Water Works

"I can't inspect the home if the water isn't on," I said to the agent on the phone.

"Right, of course. I'll have the owner turn it on for the inspection."

Several days later I exited the truck and zipped up my jacket. The wind was bitter cold. The six-thousand-square-foot home was elegant against the golf course backdrop with two-story tall pillars at the entrance.

A mansion.

I pulled my coat collar up and began the outside walk-around as the agent arrived.

The agent unlocked the imposing front door and we entered the foyer of the home. The thick cream-colored carpet underfoot smelled moldy and seemed to suck our feet into it. We looked around before moving.

"Do you hear something?" I asked.

"No. What?"

"I must be imagining it. Never mind. I'll start at the top floor and work down."

"Okay. I'll plug into power here in the foyer and get some work done. The place needs to be aired out, it smells like something died in here."

As I made my way up the immense curving staircase below an intricate crystal chandelier, I still couldn't help thinking I was hearing something in the house. A hum or gurgling, I wasn't sure which.

I forgot about it as I tested outlets and fixtures. I noted that the water pressure was weak.

I need to do a pressure test outside, I thought.

Home Inspection Answer Guide

The home was fully furnished. I noticed antiques, small statues, canopied beds, and oil paintings on the walls.

No wonder the agent wanted to be here for the inspection.

Except for the low water pressure, all of the electrical and water fixtures tested fine on the second floor. It smelled better up there too.

As I made my way back down the *Gone with the Wind* staircase, I heard the sound again.

"I *am* hearing something. I'm going to check it out." I said to the agent. "Come on with me, you can tell me if you hear anything."

We rounded the corner to the huge living room with eighteen-foot ceilings and then on to the kitchen.

"Yes, I do hear something now," said the agent.

The sound was creepy. It was a gurgling, a lapping, a swishing sound. We stopped, looking at each other. Our eyes darted to the corners of the room. The sound echoed through the hallway.

I moved over to a door in the corner of the kitchen. *This should lead to the basement.*

I looked at the agent one more time and then opened the door. The sound spilled out in a rush and I immediately knew what it was but was afraid to look. I motioned for the agent to come over.

I opened the door all the way and flicked on the light switch.

"Oh my God!" we both cried in unison.

A dark pool of water was lapping a quarter of the way up the carpeted staircase to the basement. Waves gurgled under the lower-level wall. Items floating in the pool were banging against each other and there were hissing noises and bubbles curling up from below.

I dropped my inspection belt on the kitchen floor and ran through the living room to the foyer and then to the outside. Running into the well shed, I found the supply handle and turned it to OFF.

Returning to the house, I found the agent sitting on a kitchen stool, white-faced, talking on the phone. She shook her head repeatedly.

I returned to the top of the basement stairs. The pool seemed calmer now that the water supply was off.

Ending the call, the agent came over to me as I was snapping pictures.

"What you see down there is the equivalent of a residential in ground-pool. I'm surmising a burst pipe that's been going for days in the basement, I said.

"No one is going to believe this," she said.

"No wonder the water pressure was low," I replied.

The Obsidian Cavern

When inspecting homes, ordinary doors can provide a surprise. Some doors lead to rooms, some doors lead to a dark void, and some doors are curiously locked. Sometimes you get all three.

I was inspecting a large vacation home north of Cashiers on a wide, fast-running creek. It was full of boulders, twists and turns, and waterfalls. If I had not been on a schedule, I would have stopped by the creek and pulled out my lunch box. It was a magnificent and radiant landscape. The drive to the home was narrow and steep, leading to a heavy gate. The remote the agent gave me worked, and the gates slowly opened on complaining hinges.

The house was beautifully built into the side of granite and quartz ledges, with stunning floor-to-ceiling windows. Although the home had a small footprint—perhaps two thousand square feet—two stories towered upwards, taking advantage of the very steep lot. The home had been foreclosed on and was now vacant.

What a shame. My dream house.

The first part of the inspection on the first floor revealed no anomalies. I started up the stairs to inspect the second floor and noticed a door with a deadbolt lock. When you see something like this, owners are usually trying to protect something. Normally I note in the report that I could not access the closet or room, but in this case, the bank was the owner and I doubted that they knew anything about this locked door.

I quickly got on the phone to the real estate agent.

"I'll call the bank," she said.

Three minutes later the phone rang. "No one has a key to that door. If we did, I'd say enter and report what you find. Can you pick it?"

"I'm no locksmith," I replied. "No problem, I'll put it in my report that I had to skip it."

I'm curious.

I ran my hand across the top of the door trim which is where I *hide* a key. My fingers encountered an object with Velcro stuck to the trim. A key. I put the key in the lock and tried rotating it. It worked! Leaving the key in the tumbler, I turned the knob and opened the door.

A black void.

I pulled out my flashlight and aimed it into the area. A black metal circular staircase came into view. Now I felt like Nancy Drew. I started slowly down the narrow stairs. Then I heard the door shut above. Startled, I looked up. I noticed the door had a self-closing spring.

Does it self-lock, too? I wondered.

That's all I needed was to be trapped in the remote home in a strange room with a circular staircase leading to who-knows-where. I pulled out my phone, wondering if I still had a cell signal. No bars at all. Concerned, I wondered if I could get out.

I turned around and made my way back up the steps to make sure the door had not locked on me.

I grasped the knob. Locked.

Lisa, how did you get into this situation?

I used my flashlight to search the wall for a light switch. I found it and flipped it on. Light flooded the landing.

I looked at the door lock and realized that it was the lower lock, the knob lock that wasn't opening. I pulled out several business cards and slid them into the door frame, releasing the latch.

I gave a sigh of relief. I reached around the door and moved the lock lever to vertical so I could get out again.

I wondered if I should keep exploring.

Yes.

I left the landing and started back down the staircase. Halfway down I began to hear the sound of water. When I reached the bottom, my feet were on an uneven stone floor and I was in a room about six-by-six feet with two more doors in the walls. I looked around for a switch. I found it on the opposite wall. I flipped the switch and light filled the room. I was amazed to see that the walls were carved into the cliff.

One closet was a tiny space with an electrical box. The other door was locked with a deadbolt like the one upstairs.

"Oh! I left the key upstairs," I said to myself out loud. "Shoot, I'll have to go back up and get it."

I went back up the circular staircase to retrieve it. I wondered if I wasn't getting in over my head.

I'm curious and I've come this far.

I walked back down the stairs to the locked door. The key worked, and I opened the door.

Water dripped down the walls of the narrow passageway, obsidian-colored rock hewn out of the cliff face. I could see the furrows where blasting caps had been used. I was feeling uncertain. Should I keep going? The dirt path was uneven and the walls were getting narrower as I made my way carefully down the slippery incline. I heard a sort of hissing sound as my flashlight made out a heavy closed door, blocking my way. *Go back*, my brain commanded. *No, I'm curious.*

Once again, the same key worked in this heavy door. As soon as I pushed on the door I realized the hissing sound was actually water. The door squealed on its rusty hinges.

The sound of water grew stronger as I moved slowly down the cavern path. As my curiosity grew overwhelming, I heard the old door slam shut behind me. I froze, training my light back up the passage to the door.

Great. I hope I can get back out, I thought. If something happened to me down here, no one would know.

Another dozen tentative steps led me to a sudden ninety-degree turn in the cavern wall. Light splayed on the opposite wall. I made the turn.

The waterfall that was visible from inside the home was directly in front of me.

I didn't realize I'd been holding my breath and I let it all out with a big sigh. Gulping in the humid cold air, I felt relief flood over me with the mist.

Now I just need to get out of here, I thought, as I snapped pictures. "No one will believe this," I uttered to myself.

Attic Amenities

The small two-story cottage had been vacant for a year and now a buyer was interested. Everything looked fine from the outside and passed my first walk-around looking for problems.

I finished inspecting the HVAC compressor by the side of the house and felt several large raindrops on my head. I looked around. It was a sunny day with no rain. Then I looked up. As another large wet drop hit me directly in the face,

I noticed a two-inch PVC tube sticking out of the soffit on the second story.

What in the world?

Snapping pictures on telephoto mode I made note of the location.

Putting a ladder up, I climbed to the roof. Because one side was exceptionally steep, I was unable to make it over to the area where I'd seen the PVC pipe.

I'll check it out when I get inside.

I made my way through the interior rooms, and finally to the attic. Some homes have stairs, some have large square access panels, and some homes have tiny square access panels. It was my luck that day to discover a tiny access panel inside a closet that was still filled with clothing.

I dragged my multipurpose ladder into the small closet and worked at getting the panel off. I never know what I am going to find as I open up these dark spaces. One inspector I met at recurrent training said he had a nest of snakes fall on his head as he opened an attic panel. Since hearing that, I could never get the image out of my mind.

The panel suddenly popped upward, and I trained my flashlight inside. Darkness and insulation.

I placed the panel off to the left and then noticed a light bulb with a chain. I pulled it on and the bulb worked. *Halleluiah.* Thank the heavens for small favors.

Directly in front of me was a children's swimming pool about six feet in diameter and eighteen inches high. I stood up as well as I could under the roof and trained my flashlight inside the plastic. There was about six inches of dark water thick with mold. Then I noticed the PVC pipe exiting the side of the pool and running over to the soffit vent.

Ah ha! I thought about the bacteria laden drips that still matted my hair. *Ick.*

Then I trained my light on the roof interior. I saw where a flashing next to the chimney was missing, allowing water to drip into the pool.

How clever.

I moved to the back side of the pool, careful to keep my footing on the beams so as not to fall into the room below. I started snapping pictures because, once again, I guessed no one would believe the arrangement unless they saw it.

Although an effective way to keep a roof leak from entering your home, it's not a solution that I recommend.

"A comfortable house is a great source of happiness. It ranks immediately after health and a good conscience." ~ Sydney Smith

Chapter 12: The Quiz

If you'd like to have some fun and challenge yourself, take this home inspection quiz. The answers are at the end.

1. **Builders take great pains to get everything right in your custom-built home. This means:**
   A. The municipal code inspector can do the independent inspection at the end of the build
   B. Most builders will not allow independent inspections
   C. Builders already have an inspector that they use to check for defects

D. Custom homes need several independent inspections if you want to catch errors and save money

2. **To make sure termites are not in the home, an inspector will:**
   A. Gently tap on the walls at intervals to hear acoustical sound differences
   B. Pull off at least one baseboard in every room to check for termites
   C. Recommend that the client hire a licensed pest professional to inspect the home for termites
   D. Remove insulation in attic spaces to identify pests

3. **One characteristic of radon gas is:**
   A. It is lighter than air and rises to the top floor of the house
   B. If a home has high radon, it will always have it, and it's tough to lower the level
   C. It is very expensive to test for radon
   D. If an inspector tests for and finds high radon levels, it's almost always possible to bring down to safe levels

4. **When inspectors find structural deficiencies, it is most often associated with:**
   A. The decks
   B. The roof

C. The foundation
D. The attic

5. **A buyer's home inspector may get upset if:**
   A. The seller and the seller's agent want to attend the inspection
   B. The buyer and the buyer's agent want to attend the inspection
   C. They are forced to inspect the home by themselves
   D. If the buyer is unable to attend but the buyer's agent can

6. **Home inspectors are:**
   A. Specialists
   B. Former code enforcement
   C. Also home appraisers
   D. Generalists

7. **When you hire a home inspector, look for certification from a national association, such as:**
   A. National Association of Builders (NAB)
   B. American Association of Code Enforcement (AACE)
   C. Real Estate Board of Inspectors (REBI)
   D. American Society of Home Inspectors ASHI)

8. **After conducting your home inspection, the inspector will:**
   A. Assess and cost out the repairs that are needed
   B. Write a letter with a report of repairs to the seller
   C. Grade the quality of the home on a scale from A to D.
   D. Write an extensive report that will go to the person paying for it

9. **Choose an inspector with:**
   A. Recent certification
   B. Many years of experience
   C. A real estate license
   D. An appraisal license

10. **A home inspection report can be highly useful for:**
    A. A Seller
    B. An Owner
    C. A custom home builder
    D. All of the above

See the next page for answers.

Home Inspection Answer Guide

ANSWERS:

1. D. Custom homes need several independent inspections if you want to catch errors and save money.

   For custom homes, I'd have at least four home inspections. You'll likely pay a flat fee that will be about twice what a standalone inspection would cost. Inspectors love doing these and will usually give you a discount if you ask for one.

2. C. Recommend that the client hire a licensed pest professional to inspect the home for termites.

   Inspectors will not take anything apart, and wall tapping is not a scientific way to identify termite damage.

3. D. If an inspector tests for and finds high radon levels, it's almost always possible to bring down to safe levels.

   Mitigation of radon can be as simple as sealing foundation cracks and or installing a foundation vent. Active ventilation systems are also available and can bring radon levels down substantially.

4. A. The decks.

   Seventy percent of the decks I have inspected have had some kind of structural deficiency. It is usually the attachment (or lack of attachment) to the ledger board holding the deck to the house or lack of structure supporting beams and deck supports.

5. A. The seller and the seller's agent want to attend the inspection.

   It is typical for the buyer and/or buyer's agent to attend the inspection because they are hiring the inspector. If the seller and the seller's agent show up, it could create an awkward situation with everyone asking questions.

6. D. Generalists.

   Inspectors may have a varied set of credentials and backgrounds, but the hallmark of a good inspection is a high-level review of all the systems and components.

7. D. American Association of Home Inspectors (ASHI). There are others, notably the International Association of Certified Home

Inspectors (InterNACHI). About 35 states now require licensing and recurrent training.

8. D. Write an extensive report that will go to the person paying for it.

   The report that you are paying your inspector for belongs to you and the inspector. You are not required to share it with anyone else.

9. B. Many years of experience.

   It's a given that you want to hire an inspector with credentials—state licensing if required, and association membership. But the years of experience are the most important because of the range of knowledge it gives an inspector. Years of experience also give an inspector a balanced view of defects in the home. New inspectors can be picky, and overly concerned about structural defects, and not choose the most appropriate wording to describe defects. New inspectors may also rush to judgement and call for unnecessary specialist inspections that could be costly.

10. D. All of the above

    A home inspection report will be useful over the long term to whoever orders it. For owners, a periodic home inspection can reduce surprise maintenance costs.

How did you do?

If you got eight or more correct, then award yourself an A. If you got six to seven correct, then award yourself a B, and if you got three to five correct, then award yourself a C. If you got less than three correct, then let me know so I can re-write this book.

You can find quizzes and articles on my website: https://housekeysbylisaturner.com/free-advice

"A prudent question is one-half of wisdom." ~ Francis Bacon

Questions and Answers

Everything You Wanted to Know About Home Inspection but Were Afraid to Ask

What is a home inspection?

A home inspection is an evaluation of the visible and accessible systems and components of a home (plumbing, heating and cooling, electrical, structure, roof, etc.) and is intended to give the client (buyer, seller, or homeowner) a better understanding of the home's general condition.

Most often it is a buyer who requests an inspection of the home he or she is serious about purchasing. A home inspection delivers data so that decisions about the purchase can be confirmed or questioned, and can uncover serious and expensive to repair defects that the seller/owner may not be aware of. It is not an appraisal of the property's value; nor does it address the cost of repairs. It does not guarantee that the home complies with local building codes or protect a client in the event an item inspected fails in the future.

A home inspection should not be considered a "technically exhaustive" evaluation, but rather an evaluation of the property on the day it is inspected, taking into consideration normal wear and tear for the home's age and location.

A home inspection can also include, for extra fees, radon gas testing, water testing, energy audits, pest inspections, pool inspections, and several other specific items that may be indigenous to the region of the country where the inspection takes place.

Home inspections can be used by a seller before listing the property to see if there are any hidden problems, and also by homeowners simply wishing to care for their homes, prevent surprises, and keep the home investment value as high as possible.

Home Inspection Answer Guide

The important results to pay attention to in a home inspection are:

1. Major defects, such as large differential cracks in the foundation; structure out of level or plumb; decks not installed or supported properly, etc. These are items that are expensive to fix. We classify major items as requiring more than 2 percent of the purchase price to repair.
2. Things that could lead to major defects—a roof flashing leak that could get bigger, damaged downspouts that could cause backup and water intrusion, or a support beam that was not tied in to the structure properly.
3. Safety hazards, such as exposed electrical wiring, lack of Ground Fault Circuit Interrupters (GFCI) in kitchens and bathrooms, lack of safety railing on decks more than 30 inches off the ground, etc.

Your inspector will advise you about what to do about these problems. He/she may recommend evaluation—and on serious issues most certainly will—by licensed or certified professionals who are specialists in the defect areas. For example, your inspector will recommend you call a licensed building or structural engineer if they find sections of the home that are out of alignment, as this could indicate a serious structural deficiency.

Home inspections are only done by a buyer after they sign a contract, right?

Not always. A home inspection can be used for interim inspections in new construction, as a maintenance tool by a current homeowner, a proactive technique by sellers to make their home more sellable, and by buyers wanting to determine the condition of the potential home. Sellers, in particular, can benefit from getting a home inspection before listing the home.

Here are just a few of the advantages for the seller:

- The seller knows the home. The home inspector will be able to get answers to his/her questions on the history of any problems they find.
- A home inspection will help the seller be more objective when it comes to setting a fair price on the home.
- The seller can take the report and make it into a marketing piece for the home.
- The seller will be alerted to any safety issues found in the home before they open it up for showing.
- The seller can make repairs leisurely instead of being in a rush after the contract is signed.

See Chapter 2 for more information on seller inspections.

Why should I get a home inspection?

Your new home has dozens of systems and over ten thousand parts—from heating and cooling to ventilation and appliances. When these systems and appliances work together, you experience comfort, energy savings, and durability. Weak links in the system, however, can produce assorted problems leading to a loss in value, and a shortened component life. Would you buy a used car without a qualified mechanic looking at it? Your home is far more complicated, and to have a thorough inspection that is documented in a report arms you with substantial information on which to make decisions.

Do home inspectors inspect condominium units?

Yes, and it's a good idea. When you buy a unit in a condominium, you are responsible for maintenance in your own unit. In my experience inspecting condo apartments, there's as much in a single living unit that can go wrong as there is in a home. Having common areas evaluated too will reveal how well the association is keeping up with necessary maintenance.

You can get a full inspection, which covers both the interior unit condition and condition of the common areas, or just the unit condition inspection. A full inspection will include crawl spaces and attics that attach directly to a unit.

The inspector will also assess basements, garages, common-use zones and the roof. Although you are not responsible for common areas, their condition is a clue to future assessments.

Inspection items include:

- Walls and floors for cracks, warping, and water damage
- Smoke alarms and safety features
- Water pressure
- Appliances
- Electrical systems
- HVAC
- Plumbing systems
- Windows and doors
- Patios, balconies, and shared decks
- Common areas general condition

Given the discoveries in buildings displaying poor condition in areas of high wear and tear (such as the Florida coast), it makes sense to spend some time reviewing not only the soundness of a particular condo unit but the soundness of the condominium association. Is there enough financial reserve to cover maintenance? Your inspector will review what they discovered with you materially, but then it's your job to dig into the condition of the board. What you want to avoid is a massive future assessment that will trap you financially.

Before you make your buying decision on a condominium unit:

- Get a full unit inspection. Your agent can recommend a qualified inspector.
- Review several years' worth of annual meeting minutes. Are reserves sufficient to take care of future maintenance? The condo building that collapsed in south Florida in 2021—Champlain Towers South—needed fifteen million dollars of repairs according to a letter sent by the association's president before the collapse, but the board had only seven hundred thousand dollars in reserves.[3]
- Review public records. Is there any construction defect litigation pending? Building code violations? Enforcement actions?
- Review the association bylaws. This will tell you what level of insurance you will need.

Your agent will be able to refer you to professionals who can help you do this research. Just as you would do with a free-standing home, you want to make sure that you are adequately

---

[3] Friedman, Robyn A., 2021. "A New Focus on Due Diligence." *The Wall Street Journal,* July 16, 2021, M10.

insured against unforeseen events as well as surprises.

Why can't I do the inspection myself?

Most homebuyers lack the knowledge, skill, and objectivity needed to inspect a home themselves. By using the services of a professional home inspector, they gain a better understanding of the condition of the property. This includes whether any items do not *function as intended* or *adversely affect the habitability of the dwelling* or *warrant further investigation* by a specialist. Remember that the home inspector is a generalist and is broadly trained in every home system.

Why can't I ask a family member who is handy or who is a contractor to inspect my new home?

Although your nephew or aunt may be very skilled, he or she is not trained or experienced in professional home inspections and lacks the specialized test equipment and knowledge required for an inspection. Home inspection training and expertise represent a distinct, licensed profession that employs rigorous standards of practice. Most contractors and other trade professionals hire a professional home inspector to inspect their own homes when they purchase a home.

What does a home inspection cost?

Fees are based on size, age and other aspects of the home. Inspection fees from a certified professional home inspector generally start under five hundred dollars. What you should pay attention to is not the fee, but the qualifications of your inspector. Are they nationally certified (passed the NHIE exam)? Are they state certified if required? How many years of experience do they have? I'd also advise against choosing an inspector with less than two years of experience; they may drive you crazy on the details. See Chapter 6: Choosing in Inspector.

How long does the inspection take?

This depends upon the size and condition of the home. You can usually figure an hour and a half for every thousand square feet. For example, a three-thousand-square-foot house would take about three hours. If the company also produces the report at your home, that will take an additional thirty to sixty minutes.

Do all homes require a home inspection?

Yes and no. Although not required by law in most states, I think that any buyer not getting a home inspection is doing themselves a disservice. They may find themselves with costly and unpleasant surprises after moving into the home and suffer financial headaches that could have been avoided.

Should I be at the inspection?

It's a great idea for you to be present during the inspection—whether you are a buyer, seller, or homeowner. You won't annoy the inspector if you show up near the end of their work, and they will appreciate your attention. See Chapter 1: What Buyers Need to Know.

Read the inspection agreement carefully so you understand what is covered and what is not covered in the inspection. If there is a problem with the inspection or the report, you should raise the issues quickly by calling the inspector, usually within 24 hours.

If you want the inspector to return after the inspection to show you things, this can be arranged and is a good idea. But you may be paying for the inspector's time on a return walkthrough.

Should the seller attend the home inspection that has been ordered by the buyer?

The seller will be welcome at the inspection (after all, it is their home), although they should understand that the inspector is working for the buyer. The conversation that the inspector has with the buyer may be upsetting to the seller if the seller was unaware of the items being pointed out, and the seller may be overly emotional about any defects that are found. This is one reason why the seller might want to consider getting their own inspection before listing the home.

Agents will typically advise their seller clients to not be at the home during the inspection. I think this is a good idea because it avoids awkward situations.

Can a house fail a home inspection?

No. A home inspection is an examination of the current condition of a home. It is not an appraisal, which determines market value, or a municipal inspection, which verifies local code compliance. A home inspector, therefore, cannot pass or fail a house. The inspector will objectively describe the home's physical condition and indicate which items are in need of repair or replacement.

What is included in the inspection?

The following list is not exhaustive. Not all of these are in all inspections, but the inspector will be following a standardized checklist for the home.

- Site drainage and grading
- Driveway
- Entry Steps, handrails
- Decks
- Masonry

- Landscape (as it relates to the home)
- Retaining walls
- Roofing, flashings, chimneys, and attic
- Eaves, soffits, and fascias
- Walls, doors, windows, patios, walkways
- Foundation, basement, and crawlspaces
- Garage, garage walls, floor, and door operation
- Kitchen appliances (dishwasher, range/oven/cooktop/hoods, microwave, disposal, trash compactor)
- Laundry appliances (washer and dryer)
- Ceilings, walls, floors
- Kitchen counters, floors, and cabinets
- Windows and window gaskets
- Interior doors and hardware
- Plumbing systems and fixtures
- Electrical system, panels, entrance conductors
- Electrical grounding, GFCI, outlets
- Smoke (fire) detectors
- Ventilation systems and insulation
- Heating equipment and controls
- Ducts and distribution systems
- Fireplaces
- Air Conditioning and controls
- Heat Pumps and controls
- Safety items such as means of egress, TPRV valves, railings, etc.

Other items that are not a part of the standard inspection can often be added for an additional fee. Many of these inspections must be performed by licensed professionals other than the home inspector. See Chapter 9, Additional Inspections.

- Radon Gas Test (if your home falls in a high radon area)
- Water Quality Test
- Termite Inspection
- Gas Line Leak Test
- Sprinkler System Test
- Swimming Pool and Spa Inspection
- Mold
- Septic System Inspection
- Alarm System

Your inspector will work with other companies on some of these specialized inspections. You should ask about the arrangement and what extra fees will be involved.

What is not included in the inspection?
Most people assume that everything is inspected in depth on inspection day. This misunderstanding has caused many a homebuyer to be upset with their inspector.

If you hired someone with licenses for heating and cooling, electrical, plumbing, engineering, etc. to inspect your house, it would take about sixteen hours and cost you thousands of dollars. It is much more practical to hire a professional inspector who has generalist knowledge of home systems, knows what to look for, and can recommend further inspection by a specialist if needed.

Your inspector is also following very specific guidelines as he/she inspects your home. These are either national guidelines (ASHI - American Society of Home Inspectors, InterNACHI - International Association of Certified Home Inspectors) or state guidelines.

These guidelines are carefully written to protect both your home and the inspector. Here are some examples.

We are specifically directed to not turn systems on if they were off at the time of the inspection (such as a propane tank); we are not allowed to move furniture (might harm something); not allowed to turn on water if it is off (possible flooding), and not allowed to break through a sealed attic hatch (possible damage).

The downside of this practice is that by not operating a control, by not seeing under the furniture, and not getting into the attic or crawlspace, we might miss identifying a problem. However, put into perspective, the chances of missing something serious because of these rules are quite low, and the guideline as it relates to safety and not harming anything in the home is a good one.

There are other items that 95 percent of inspectors consider outside a normal inspection, and these include inspecting most things that are not bolted down (installed in the home) such as electronics, low voltage lighting, space heaters, portable air conditioners, or specialized systems such as water purifiers and alarm systems.

What if there are things you can't inspect (like snow on the roof)?

It just so happens that some days the weather elements interfere with a full home inspection. If there is snow on the roof the inspector will tell you they were unable to inspect it. They will be looking at the eves and the attic, and any other areas where they can get an idea of condition, but the inspector will write in the report that he/she could not inspect the roof. It may be impractical to return another day once the snow melts because inspectors have full schedules. However, you can usually pay an inspector a small fee to return and inspect the one or two items they were unable to inspect when they were there the first time. This is just the way things go. If you ask the inspector for a re-inspection, they will usually inspect the items then at no extra charge (beyond the re-inspection fee).

Will the inspector walk on the roof?

The inspector will walk on the roof if it is safe, accessible, and strong enough so that there is no damage done to it by walking on it. Some roofs, such as slate and tile, should not be walked on. Sometimes, because of poor weather conditions, extremely steep roofs, or very high roofs, the inspector will not be able to walk the roof. The inspector will try to get up to the edge though, and will also use binoculars where accessibility is a problem. They will also examine the roof from the upper windows if that is possible. There is a lot the inspector can determine from a visual examination from a ladder and from the ground, and they will be able to tell a lot more from inside the attic about the condition of the roof. This is a situation where a drone camera is handy. More and more inspectors are using drone cams for roof inspections.

Should I have my house tested for Radon? What exactly is Radon?

In many areas of the country, the answer is a definite yes. You can ask your real estate agent about this or go on to the internet for a radon map of the country. Radon is a colorless, odorless, and tasteless radioactive gas that's formed during the natural breakdown of uranium in soil, rock, and water. Radon exits the ground and can seep into your home through cracks and holes in the foundation. Radon gas can also contaminate well water.

Health officials have determined that radon gas is a serious carcinogen that can cause lung cancer, second only to cigarette smoking. The only way to find out if your house contains radon gas is to perform a radon measurement test, which your home inspector can do. Make sure the person conducting your test has been trained to The National Environmental Health Association (NEHA) or The National Radon Safety Board (NRSB) standards. See Chapter 10: Radon Facts, for more information.

What about a newly constructed home? Does it need a home inspection?

Yes. In fact, inspectors find far more problems, some quite serious, in newly constructed homes. This is not due to your builder's negligence—he/she has done the best job they could with subcontractors and planning—it's just that there are so many systems in a home it is close to impossible to inspect everything and correct it before the Certificate of Occupancy (CO) is issued.

I recommend getting several professional home inspections near the completion stages of the home to discover everything that should be corrected. See Chapter 5: What Builders Need to Know.

If the house is still new but has been sitting for a while before the sale, it's even more important to get a home inspection. I have seen water lines not hooked up, plumbing lines not hooked up, sewer lines not hooked up, vents not hooked up, and a variety of other serious but easily correctable problems.

I am having a home built. The builder assures me he will inspect everything. Should I have an independent inspector make periodic inspections?

Absolutely yes. No matter how good your builder is, he/she will miss things. They are so concerned with the house, they get so close to their work, as do the subcontractors, that important items can, and will be, overlooked. Have a professional inspector make at least four interim inspections. The money will be well spent.

What is the Pre-Inspection Agreement?

Most service professionals have a service agreement, and home inspection is no different. There is enough confusion about what a home inspection should deliver that the agreement is important. Some homeowners who get a home inspection expect everything in the home to be perfect after they took care of the major defects. Imagine getting a call from a homeowner a year later who says the toilet is not flushing—

remember that the inspection is a moment in time snapshot.

In the inspection agreement, the inspector is clear about what the inspection delivers and the things that are not covered, as well as what you should do if you are not pleased with the services. By reviewing this beforehand you will understand much more about the inspection and be happier with the results.

A home inspection does not guard against future problems, nor does it guarantee that all problems will be found.

What kind of report will I get following the inspection?

There are as many versions of a "report" as there are inspection companies. Guidelines dictate that the inspector deliver a written report to the client. This can range from a handwritten checklist that has multiple press copies without pictures to a computer-generated and professionally produced report with digital pictures 35 pages long and can be converted to Adobe PDF for storage and emailing.

Check with your inspector about the report he or she uses. I recommend the computer-generated report since the checklist is more detailed and easier for the homeowner /buyer/seller to detail out the issues with photographs. In this technical era, the reports must be web accessible and emailable to match the technologies most of us are using.

There are some great things you can use the report for in addition to the wealth of information it simply gives you on your new home.

Use the report as a checklist and guide for the contractor to make repairs and improvements or get estimates and quotes from more than one contractor.

Use the report as a budgeting tool using the inspector's recommendations and the remaining expected life of components to keep the property in top shape.

If you are a seller, use the report to make repairs and improvements, raising the value of the home and impressing the buyers. Then have a re-inspection and use this second report as a marketing tool for prospective buyers.

Use the report as a punch list on a re-inspection and as a baseline for ongoing maintenance. See Chapter 8: How to Use the Report.

Will the report be emailable or available as an Adobe PDF file?

Yes. The more electronic and accessible, the better.

Are home inspection reports on the public record?

No, home inspection reports are not public record. Home inspection reports are confidential and owned by the client who hired the home inspector and paid for the home inspection. The client can choose to share (or not share) a copy of the home inspection report with anyone of their choosing.

What if I think the inspector missed something?

Inspectors are human, and yes, they do miss items. However, they routinely use advanced tools and techniques to reduce the possibility that they will miss something. This includes detailed checklists, reference manuals, computer-based lists, and a methodical 'always-done-the-same-way' of physically moving around your home. That is one of the reasons that an inspector can miss an item when they get interrupted. The inspector will have a set way of resuming the inspection if this happens. If, in the end, something IS missed, call the inspector and discuss it. It may warrant the inspector returning to view something that you found. Remember, the inspector is doing the very best job they know how to do, and probably did not miss the item because they were lax in their technique or did not care. When I was an inspector, I always returned to look at something at no charge if the client asked.

Will the inspector look for lead, asbestos, and Chinese drywall?

Lead and asbestos are found in some properties built prior to 1978. By now most of these homes have been remediated. If you are concerned, ask your inspector for advice. They can refer you to a professional.

Chinese drywall was installed in the U.S. between 2001 and 2008; most of the affected homes were built during 2006 and 2007. By now most of these homes have been fully remediated. Chinese drywall was made at the time with contaminants and smelled strongly of the chemical sulfur. If you have a concern, ask your inspector for advice.

What if the inspector tells me I should have a professional engineer or a licensed plumber or contractor in to look at something they found? Isn't this "passing the buck"?

You may be disappointed that further investigation is required, but your inspector is doing exactly the right thing. The purpose of the inspection is to discover defects that affect your safety and the functioning of the home; the inspector is a generalist, not a specialist.

The inspection code of ethics as well as national and state guidelines dictate that only contractors licensed in their specialty field should work on these systems and areas. When they tell you that a specialist is needed, there may be a bigger, more critical issue that you need to know about.

If you move into the home without getting these areas checked by a qualified specialist, you could be in for some nasty and expensive surprises. The inspector doesn't want to cause you any more expense or worry, so when they do recommend further evaluation, they are being serious about protecting you and your investment.

Will the inspector provide a warranty on the inspected items?

Most inspectors do not give the homeowner a warranty on inspected items. Remember, a home inspection is a visual examination on a certain day, and the inspector cannot predict what issues could arise over time after the inspection. However, some inspectors are now including a service warranty from one of the home warranty companies in the United States on the inspected items for sixty or ninety days. This is a good deal, and the agreement can be extended after the initial period for a relatively small amount of money.

If your inspector does not give you a warranty from one of the major companies providing them, you can go online and find one to suit your budget. They are renewable year to year. Make sure you understand what kind of coverage they will give you, and if there is any co-pay on repairs.

A home warranty is not an insurance policy, but rather a service contract that pays the cost of repair or replacement of covered items, such as major kitchen appliances, as well as electrical, plumbing, heating and air conditioning systems. These warranties don't cover windows, doors, roofing, or other structural items.

Do most inspection companies offer money back guarantees?

Most inspection companies do not offer a satisfaction guarantee nor do they mention it in their advertising. It's always a good thing if you can get extra services for no additional cost from your inspection company, and of course, a satisfaction guarantee is an indication of superior customer service. You usually have to call your inspection company right after the inspection to tell them you are not satisfied.

If you're not happy with the services, you should talk to your inspector first. They will usually bend over backward to please you, including returning to the home to check something out. Give them this chance.

When I ran my own inspection company, I did offer a 100 percent money-back guarantee to customers, and I had less than half a percent of customers ask for it. The few who did ask had misunderstood what I was inspecting (for example, thought the inspection covered termites). That was my error in not explaining it well enough.

What if my report comes back with nothing really defective in the home? Should I ask for my money back?

No, don't ask for your money back—you just received great news. Now you can complete your home purchase with peace of mind about the condition of the property and all its equipment and systems.

You will have valuable information about your new home from the inspector's report and will want to keep that information for future reference. Most importantly, you can feel assured that you are making a well-informed purchase decision.

What if the inspection reveals serious defects?

If the inspection reveals serious defects in the home (I define a serious defect as something that will cost more than 2 percent of the purchase price to fix), then pat yourself on the back for getting an inspection. You just saved yourself a ton of money. Of course, it is disappointing, even heart-wrenching, to find out that your well-researched house is now a problem house, but you now know the facts and can either negotiate with the seller or move on. You may want the home so much that it will be worth it to negotiate the price and then perform the repairs. Imagine, though, if you had not gotten the inspection—you would have had some very unpleasant surprises.

Can I ask my home inspector to perform the repairs?

You can, but if your inspector is ethical, he/she will refuse, and correctly so; it is a conflict of interest for the person who inspected your home to also repair it. Inspectors are specifically barred from this practice by licensing authorities, and it's a good rule—an inspector must remain completely impartial when he or she inspects your home.

This is one reason you should have a professional home inspector inspect your home and not a contractor—the contractor will want the repair work and you are likely to not have an objective inspection from this person even though they mean well and are technically competent.

Does the Seller have to make the repairs?

The inspection report results do not place an obligation on the seller to repair everything mentioned in the report. Once the home condition is known, the buyer can work with their agent to ask the seller for concessions. It could be a discount on the price, or it could be fixing what's wrong in the house. The report will be clear about what is a repair and what is a discretionary improvement. This area should be negotiated between the parties.

It's important to know that the inspector must stay out of this discussion because it is outside of their scope of work.

After the home inspection and consulting with the seller on the repairs, can I re-employ the inspector to come re-inspect the home to make sure everything got fixed?

You certainly can, and it's a good idea. For a fee, the inspector will return to determine if the repairs were completed and if they were completed correctly.

What if I find problems after I move into my new home?

A home inspection is not a guarantee that problems won't develop after you move in. However, if you believe that a problem was visible at the time of the inspection and should have been mentioned in the report, your first step should be to call the inspector. He or she will be fine with this and does want you to call if you think there is a problem. If the issue is not resolved with a phone call, the inspector will come to your home to look at it, and they should not charge you for this review. They will want you to be satisfied and will do everything they can to achieve this goal.

One way to protect yourself between the inspection and the move-in is to conduct a final walkthrough on closing day and use both the inspection report and a walkthrough checklist to make sure everything is as it should be.

How has home inspection changed in the last twenty years?

The fundamentals remain the same, but the tools have improved substantially. Inspectors used to always walk the roof. While they still can, they may substitute a drone cam for areas they cannot see well.

Inspectors can now use robot cams to enter what they consider dangerous spaces. This includes attics and crawlspaces.

Some inspectors now use sophisticated infrared detection and tiny cameras to discover hidden moisture and other problems.

If you enjoyed this book, would you rate it on Amazon and/or Goodreads?

Ratings help sell books, and a portion of the proceeds go to the non-profit *Western Carolina Youth Aviation Foundation* to help kids discover careers in aviation. **WCYAF.org**

Thank you!

INDEX

Agents 21
Alarm Systems 59
American Society of Home Inspectors . 44, 83, 102
Appraisers 43, 44, 83
Asbestos 110
Building contract 35
Building inspectors ... 34
Buyers .... i, vii, 5, 98
Chimney 60
Chinese drywall 110
City building inspector 34, 43
Condominium units .. 93
Creosote 60
Custom home 31, 36, 37, 84
Decks 82
Drones 46
Energy Recovery System 38
ERV 38, 39
Gas appliances 39
Home builders 32
Home components life expectancy 17
Home inspection report .xii, 25, 43, 55, 84, 88, 109
HVAC ..7, 16, 17, 65, 77, 94
Independent inspections 35, 37, 81, 82, 85
Indoor Air Quality 59
Inspection fees 97
Inspection reports .. 109
International Association of Certified Home Inspectors. 17, 44, 87, 102
Lawn Sprinklers 59
Lead 110
Maintenance advice 7
Major defects 26, 54, 91, 106
Material defect disclosure 54
Missed something ... 109
Mold inspection 59
Molds 59
Owners 15
Pest professional 8, 58, 82, 85
Plumbing vents 27
Pools and spas 60
Pre-Inspection Agreement 106
Radon ..9, 13, 58, 61, 62, 63, 64, 82, 85, 90, 101, 104, 105
Repairs 115

Safety hazards............ 91
Seller inspections.... 14, 28, 92
Sellers........................... 11
Septic systems............ 59
Service manual 17
Social media 45
Social Media 47
Specialists 26, 28, 57, 91

Structural engineer .. 34, 91
Structural Inspection 60
Termite............. 8, 49, 85
Warranty ... 37, 111, 112
Water heater....... 15, 43
Water testing 58, 90
WDO 8, 58

LISA TURNER

Home Inspection Answer Guide is Lisa's fifth book. For information and free articles, go to: https://dreamtakeflight.com/lisa-turner-books

In ***Team Steps Guide to Problem Solving***, her first business management book (2015, Turner Creek), Lisa reveals the shortcuts to solve problems on the production floor—and in life itself. In her career as a manufacturing engineer, Lisa saved thousands of dollars that were being spent unnecessarily by eliminating waste in the manufacturing process.

Two years later, in ***House Keys – The Essential Homeowner's Guide*** (2017, Turner Creek),

Lisa took her problem-solving principles into the area of home inspection. In her career as a home inspector and general contractor, she discovered and wrote about all the things that builders were missing or doing wrong in home construction. She's saving homeowners thousands of dollars now by revealing the tips and tricks to get a great home built for a small price, and time and money-saving tricks on home maintenance and home organization.

Switching gears, Lisa decided to write her own story in **Dream Take Flight** (2019, Turner Creek). In this story full of adventures, Lisa "breaks the rules" for women in the 1970s, working high-rise construction as a trim carpenter and starting a bicycle shop. She goes on to build an airplane in her garage, flying the small airplane from Florida to Maine and back and reconciles with her family in the process.

The theme that runs through Lisa Turner's life is one of high achievement born of the ability to choose the most important things to work on. At the end of her memoir is a goal-setting section that high schools are now using to help students discover values and set goals that are achievable and meaningful.

She carried this over into her next book, **Your Simplest Life** (2020, Turner Creek), where you can learn the secrets that Lisa uses to "get things done" and make sure they are the right things that bring happiness and joy to life every single day.

Visit Lisa's Author Page:
https://www.amazon.com/Lisa-Turner/e/B018O79HFO

Facebook: https://www.facebook.com/LisaTurnerBooks/

"The purpose of life, after all, is to live it, to taste experience to the utmost, to reach out eagerly and without fear for newer and richer experience." ~ Eleanor Roosevelt

Notes

Lisa Turner

Complimentary Quizzes and Articles

House Keys Free

https://housekeysbylisaturner.com/free-advice

www.ingramcontent.com/pod-product-compliance
Lightning Source LLC
Chambersburg PA
CBHW021951160426
43209CB00001B/3